C700651640

CEN 06/11

D1362585

libraries ni

Please return this item by the date above.
You can renew it at any library, or via call-point
028 9032 7515, or online
www.librariesni.org.uk

Rachael Boast

Sidereal

PICADOR

First published 2011 by Picador
an imprint of Pan Macmillan, a division of Macmillan Publishers Limited
Pan Macmillan, 20 New Wharf Road, London N1 9RR
Basingstoke and Oxford
Associated companies throughout the world
www.panmacmillan.com

ISBN 978-0-330-51339-5

Copyright © Rachael Boast 2011

The right of Rachael Boast to be identified as the
author of this work has been asserted by her in accordance
with the Copyright, Designs and Patents Act 1988.

All rights reserved. No part of this publication may be
reproduced, stored in or introduced into a retrieval system, or
transmitted, in any form, or by any means (electronic, mechanical,
photocopying, recording or otherwise) without the prior written
permission of the publisher. Any person who does any unauthorized
act in relation to this publication may be liable to criminal
prosecution and civil claims for damages.

9 8 7 6 5 4 3 2 1

A CIP catalogue record for this book is available from
the British Library.

Printed in the UK by CPI Mackays, Chatham ME5 8TD

This book is sold subject to the condition that it shall not,
by way of trade or otherwise, be lent, re-sold, hired out,
or otherwise circulated without the publisher's prior consent
in any form of binding or cover other than that in which
it is published and without a similar condition including this
condition being imposed on the subsequent purchaser.

Visit www.picador.com to read more about all our books
and to buy them. You will also find features, author interviews and
news of any future events, and you can sign up for e-newsletters
so that you're always first to hear about our new releases.

LIBRARIES NI	
C700651640	
RONDO	27/05/2011
821.92	£ 8.99
CENDER	

To my Mother and Father,
with love and gratitude

Contents

Lank Space, and scytheless Time with branny hands
Barren and soundless as the measuring sands,
Not mark'd by flit of Shades, – unmeaning they
As moonlight on the dial of the day!

S.T. Coleridge, *Limbo*, 1811

Sidereal

I

Human Telescope

Anything to overwhelm
your own thoughts and feelings,
you took to touring the waterfalls –
Lodore, Moss Force, Scale Force –
for their savage sounds.

And as those water-slopes drowned out
any hope of appropriate love
by dramatizing how out of hand it was,
perhaps you dreamt back that evening
in 1781, looking up at the planets and stars,

thinking about the erratic orbit of Uranus,
your young mind getting it, of course,
being already *habituated to the Vast*.
So thank god for a district where shadows
loomed larger than your own desires,

for the new addition to the cosmos,
allowing you the space to consider
how change and sameness, concurrent,
might absolve you
even in the ongoing downfall.

On Reading Lowell's Imitations of Sappho

What is nearest at hand . . . these nerves
in my fingertips are eyes, five pairs of eyes
pressing the pillow where your head might lie,
looking for your face, one day. Time,

now and then, allows for intimation
that abides like the rings around Saturn.
I can easily make you understand this
for it's not love that's evasive,

it's the years spent void of course,
perfecting a face in the empty mirrors
of memory. Yet all those rooms I slept in
I know now their corners were touching;

each echoed where I'd already been
until I could see through the walls, just as a poem
when at last it finds its true form
seems as though it's been written before.

Fire Shower

Lying down on a bench by the bridge,
a moon in late Gemini hidden from view,
I think of you who I loved a moment ago
as handfuls of light thrown up in the sky
find the brief flower of their suspension.

They fall so much shorter
than those on-lookers of the upper air;
our old loves, our oarsmen, radiant
in their silence, too steady to take an insult,
too self-possessed to need us.

Lights from regal crescents, Brunel's
ingenious shortcut to the woods
and rockets fired from the observatory roof
leave me cold – my eye's on Jupiter, just visible
through the cloud: *first you see me, now you don't.*

Attic

My head bowed under the rafters
I make a start in the attic's advantage,
the lowered lamp, a cushion
deleting the daylight, but I'm given
to climbing out onto the flat roof
leaving my papers, my books,
the closed doors and closed windows,
for those dark sayings
that have no hinges to swing
towards what they mean, and so
are more like song, more necessary.
I'd rise like this, day after day,
above the strain of hard angles, servant's quarters,
clarifying the openness of your face,
love, and this generous sky.

The Hum

There is not yet a single word, but the poem
can already be heard . . .
  —Osip Mandelstam

It takes all night to turn the page –
no offence to the poem – its image
sets up so bright a mirror
the room moves towards it, vaster

for all the darkness I'm left sitting in.
By mid-morning you were fathoming
how to decant me from one vessel to another,
his to yours, replace the stopper

and drink. But what you drank was laced
with a distance, like moonlight traced
back to the moon at her most explicit,
so much so you have to listen for it

close to my mouth. Then, in that way you have
when you persist, like a siderostat,
in fixing me in your view,
what I've kept hidden becomes visible to you.

And that's when the hum begins, suffusing the room
in the same way the face, when it communes
with the cup, disappears into it –
a moment in which we are only our lips.

Other Roads

I. Maps

Pitfall, quandary, threshold,

and that difficult word, 'crisis' —
but what is crisis if not crossroad,
and a sense that being lost,
even in the familiar, is a skill.

The half-cleared breakfast table
is turning into a kind of map,
the lines and echo-lines of its oak
unknot from growth marks;

small dark tellings of things
that happened against the grain,
pulse-in-wood things
that, by not being said, ring true.

The Ordnance Survey concertinas
out in front of you — a shift in scale:
punch-bowl, tumulus, causeway,
coniferous wood;

the mood lifts, assures your gravitas,
and a spirit of place
where already the day
is branching and branching out.

II. Touching Ground

Eventually I pull over,
find a flat stone, and sit looking out
at Hindhope Law, Oh Me Edge,
Monkside and Good Prospect.

My shape altering from car
to open air, coupled with the thrill
of momentum's deferral,
brings me back to my senses' best use:

a stream snug through a field,
mercurial around rock-fall,
is every bit of a cool surprise
as the suggestion

that all I need is to touch ground –
that's a big enough mystery –
and from there affirm the heavy cloud
palms down, blessing these dark

rounded hills of Northumberland,
their hoods lowered,
vowed to silence and the inhospitable,
living in praise of thistle, and Queen Anne's lace;

a whole landscape in *horarium*.

III. Altars of the North

So shy under the prolific chemistry
of shade, the wild garlic, alkanet
and sated slugs oozing out
of the after-rain, give me my bearings.

The peace almost unsettles
as I stand where you once stood,
the abbey ruins communicant,
opening up their octaves.

Onto Durham and Melrose,
and though I couldn't track or trace it,
some clean change claimed me.
Down from the throat, into the rib-vault,

it settled like snow melting into grass,
clear as a name: Aelred, Bede, Cuthbert,
an incanted cure
poured in good measure.

Peace and Plenty

Beside the low window of a rancid pub in Kendal
my bed is made for the overnight stop.
It's about half way. The car cools
in someone else's parking space;
a pint of kindness from downstairs
ticks on top of the cupboard;
the plumbing is bust;
the charity event's in full swing.

Charmed out of my socks and shoes
by soft-spoken water, I lie there thinking
of the riverbed sucking at heron's feet,
black water frothing at the drop,
and say to it: good riddance to the English apology –
give me your best elixirs and I'll be sound asleep.

Moonlight on the Dial of the Day

No one would wish a train journey on a budgerigar,
so just as well it turns out to be someone's mobile.
But now I'll be needing my portion of window –
thank you – through which to stare at the silent world:

sea villages, and fields hemmed with pink lights,
all of Nature replete in her time-trapped
opiate moment. Morning, noon and night
she's like this, a world we can never quite reach.

Administered in small doses, your messages,
barren and soundless, luminous with cold comfort,
reduce our two names to a single letter,

the same letter that marks the spot
where I've buried with branny hands
this excellent habit of love, under the earth.

Pinnacles

And as there is no chance of sleep
you'll spend the hours considering all the sounds
rain could be against the fabric of the tent:
the tuning of a radio, the static of a zillion midges,
hard applause, crumpled foil, the barking of a silver dog
who wants sometimes just to stop and not have to go on.

And you'll seek your own addition to the consensus
of the audible, until the river you're pitched by
comes to recognize your tread, the rhyming of your breath,
as you rest your ear to the ground
to track where the music's coming from,
wanting sometimes just to stop and not have to go on.

The worsening of the mountains confounds you.
They blacken, faceless, and you can't figure
how to look at them, or how to ignore them,
whether they are beautiful, or if they could cure you.
And so you lie there sighing like a slide guitar,
wanting sometimes just to stop, and not have to go on.

Agrarian Song

Mars was once considered a god of the soil,
which seems about right, given the effort
of turning it. I sang as I worked;
I sang for you; I sang to let the muscles
of my back know *this could go on all day.*

I pulled at horsetail. The hurt earth's
claim on it seemed intricate.
Its effort is the effort of resistance –
each root-node, palpably unclasped,
made for a tug-of-war with the unseen.

The effort of the earthworm contorts
his volume headlong.
Drawing the missing half of his world
down like a hood, he'd have seen stars,
pushing like that, into the pixels of his darkness.

You're taken with this muck under my nails,
these gardener's hands that crackle
along your arms like flame. Plant in me
the effort of your dark songs.
Constellate them.

Avenue of Limes

The whole place is bushed out –
mid-July heat and equipoise bodied
in the aphid's meticulous frenzy,
the song-radar of the blackbird,

and the lime tree leaves
faint with chlorophyll, bending
like rods for the cool green
tint of the streaming air.

I call out to them:
by-standing trouble-shooters,
upholders of the peace,
Seraphim of the long gravel drive,

and for once I'm off the hook,
unscrutinized,
given the all-clear,
fever lifting under the hush.

A View of Canaletto's Venice

for John

Never give a sword to a man who can't dance
  —Confucius

Precision draws your eye along the Grand Canal
as along the length of a foil

rising and falling with its flippant weight,
its back-drift and accurate intent.

From the watermark of mottled buildings
on either side, closing in to the dome

of Santa Maria della Salute, you are, at the same time,
foregrounded in broad awareness,

broad enough to imagine that your sudden cry
is like a gondola rolling on echoes;

so much so, you arrive into everywhere at once.
And this is your skill: faced one way,

then another, your wits remain sharp,
you measure yourself, as shadow measures the sun.

And this is mine: *Passata sotto* – draw your eye
along my lines, complete in their letdown and uplift.

Cycle Path

From the bottom of the pool, fixed stars
Govern a life.
  —Sylvia Plath

All the selig churches of Suffolk
lost to view, it must have seemed saner
to bike downhill that Sunday afternoon,
face lowered to avert the rain
from hitting my eyeballs; to follow
a white-flowered hedgerow into self-
forgetting, my tongue stuck
to the roof of my mouth. Calling out
along the rapid byway, my words
addressed to no one but resembling prayer
offered their long vowels to the air-waves.

And here's that pond, that sanctum,
found years ago occulted below ash and willow
where, in the local world, I saw the far-
reaching in the sun's silver shadow,
ripples from a stone. If I recall rightly,
by evening the mirrors in the trees
had diminished, as had any sense
of where I was going, or at what point
I was supposed to turn back.
Now, as before, only the dippers and skaters
can plot my fortune in the water.

Frosted Fields

So these are the veils of the morning,
the last gift to be given
by air and into air,
and by the slow sun
heavy with all the days of the year.

To say I can't get close enough
to this cold chemistry
is wrong; nor am I close
to its distance; for each way of saying
creates another veil.

So these are the veils of a landscape
that luxuriates the thought of you
as you tilt your face towards me,
looking and looking
for that shiver of peace.

View of the Gorge from the Avon

(With a copy of the *Purgatorio*)

I'm mirrored here, in this limbo,
where greys of the gorge sheer towards purple,
pick out orange, brown, rust-red.

I'd pay double to be guided past
the tectonic curvature of this glorious rift,
and fathom it for what it is.

If I had a peregrine's view, I'd say,
we think we chose our moments,
but the whole thing's synchronized.

I'd say, you're that wave – a time and a place
when the woods secrete their fragrance,
the stars their sensitization.

Blind Date

He said he structured space with light
for a living, but was unable to account
for my habits of mind that amount
only to this: a love of words that coincide
their beauty and their bite; that I'd call holy
but is perhaps diseased. After an hour we parted
under Blackfriars bridge near the book market,
and within minutes I was glad to be free,
browsing for a good line I might lift off the page
until its sonic architecture maps exactly
onto my locality. And in this way,
I eased love's stubborn *aporia*
into how it actually is, lyric and unfixed,
the water under the bridge.

Highlands

The evening rain, staccato
against the window, rehearses
for another downpour,
bringing the backpackers in to rest.
What presses on me is this:
       we have to walk a long way
       before the cloud comes down to meet us.

Glinn Chrochte, the hanging valleys
of Nevis: I should draw the line here,
across this reach of schist and wind,
the Steall Falls and the whitewater,
remember the easy climes, tell myself
       we find where we belong
       by first being lost.

But this steep drop –
this vertiginous longing –
leads, as it always must, to the stag head
mounted on the wall above the bar,
insignia of what it means
       never to turn back
       from a fork in the road,

to imagine what it's like to grow
both herald and threat of antler,
the come-on and the back-off;

to be self-possessed,
carrying nothing,
          to throw bone-lightning
          down in bog-cotton.

The Extra Mile

(The wife of Job has a re-think)

I

After three hours' kip, the day slumped
into one meandering back-drift.
She'd have slept anywhere, almost drove the car
into a ditch of primroses, so soft
in their long sunk hammock.

And as for that feeling of flight, of being
pulled over the sea into another time zone –
she'd picked that up from him,
far gone on diazepam (as aerodynamic
as ever he could be), soaring

into a well-deserved dream of the Eagle Nebula
they call *The Pillars of Creation*, so like rock,
yet so like light, possessing a rainbow-body
the way metaphor possesses a poem
without ever disclosing how it did so.

II

What kept her up into the night
was Plate XV of Blake's illustrations,
looking to see if her estranged husband
had still got the boils, or whether they'd healed,
asking herself why his gaze

wanders off out of the frame
whilst his body, in all its compressed
rigour, like a heaped cairn,
crouches in the cold tabernacle
of Yahweh's dark saying.

She realised that "curse God and die"
had only propelled him further
along the negative path, so no wonder
he hadn't looked her in the eye.
And now he was miles away.

III

Perhaps what he needed was not a second skin
in case the first was too thin.
Nor a strategy for mornings when his eyes
would weep in their rimy sockets,
having stayed open all night.

She remembers that look of his,
eyes starry as Antares,
red eye of Scorpius, and how he said
they would fire back what they'd stared at
into his bad dreams:

rings of paint on the ceiling
uncoiling into shapes of angels,
armed and opening a sky-path
to the calmest place in the storm –
which, on waking, promptly sealed over again.

IV

What's needed, he thought of first,
a new belief that broke the old code:
discomfort is corrosive,
melts apparent surfaces away
until one last question remains – how to suffer

without feeling you've lost out on anything.
So what was I good for? she laments.
His insight came of necessity,
making him the upright man
he'd only thought he was before.

Which means – in all – I was supposed
to be unhelpful. I can hear him now:
my dear, you're such a bad driver –
just keep track of the white stripe,
let it reason with you these last few miles.

V

Some things that don't happen,
Elihu had told her, in a moment of wisdom,
stop disasters from happening –
though Job had said that disaster
meant being 'out of step with the stars'.

Who to believe when Yahweh doesn't appear?
Not that he'd give a straight answer
to any of the questions that now
have her mind working in overdrive,
such as – why does the heart furl

like a winter rose, withdraw
when it means to disclose? Does he,
whose fortunes are soon to double
from eleven to twenty two, not see
how hard a part I've played in this fiasco?

VI

Such hardness only widened the distance
between them, until love's density
collapsed in on itself like a burnt-out star –
that weight that drops in the chest,
drops like a pendulum, must nevertheless

be carried lightly, or else fall further.
He was so like Flammarion's pilgrim
with his head stuck slightly out of the real
he made her laugh. But not now,
for that shining wake left behind

after Leviathan's whipped out of sight
implies we're most fecund when taken
to the edge of all we can sense,
but not encompass – just as she follows
after him, thinking, *you never know* . . .

VII

There is no other place from which empathy
can begin but in negative space.
And perhaps that's what it means
to go the extra mile,
to get the right amount of distance

between how you started out
and where you arrive. Driving back
from the airport, she started thinking aloud,
wondering if the reason Blake gave Behemoth
such a remarkably human ear was to say:

only we know creation is a brilliant atrocity.
Yes, Job replies, glancing in the wing mirror,
the point being, when we remember this, something'll give —
time, most likely — a torn veil which uneclipses
the heavenly bodies, cures the navel gaze.

Downtime

Impossible to soak in the high buildings
that line the Royal Mile while sober;
so unlike most tour guides, I always say
if you just totter along, the real map
opens out, and thereby you'll cover more ground
which leaves me free to spend an inglorious hour

below street level, a dram with a clean finish
set fair and square on the table.
No stranger to these shady paths that turn back
on themselves, I resume the business
of letting you go, giving myself
this one last porous hour to distil
thought from thought, until I can at least agree
that what we can't bear suffers our loss.

A Right Angle

Down to the level of stone,
down to the core of the city,
the sun sets off aqua-oxide
against a soft, palpable
bruise of cloud,
gold-leafed and edging away.

You watch the bobbing heads outside
roll in, become the dress and fuss
of coffee drinkers,
their faces coronal around raised cups,
and push yourself upright
in your furry chair:

to us the sun is silent, yet it roars
in the unsettled heart of its furnace,
stoked by its own self-wounding
self-hallowed chorus.
After a strong roast, you decide
it's best to bear with these dissonances,

outwit them, expect every dusk
to be heartbreaking. Last night
you dreamt of the winter bear,
Artus, asleep on the ground,
pulled all the shining buttons
off his high-collared coat, and ran.

Cipher

It was a better wine, on offer
in a shabby newsagents
you understand, and by midnight
the day just about began,
laughing off the last eleven hours

glad in a way you'd not see
those four zeros
that, for a minute, lit up the screen
with a nothingness I could count on;
for how could there be anything

less than this, yet so total?
I closed my eyes over you,
relied on the absolute invasion
of our two privacies to bury me
under the quilt cover's closing prayer.

Cabin Fever

When night and the key to the door
descend together to the bottom
of a bottle of Laphroaig,
have your good ear ready
until the firth is a salty chorale,
the moon's meadow,
or a Collect for the day that never was
quite how you'd hoped,
but better – beyond hope,
distilled from some deeper resource
of things as they are, just as they are;
Collect, also, for peace
in the faint hours that come
once the final decision to sleep
is made, then unmade,
then tossed aside;
and for *aid against peril*
by way of saying that, yes,
water is *holy desire* and *good counsel*,
possesses a body unlike other bodies,
neither singular nor plural –
and as you bed down with it
the light in the room tilts,
and begins to decant.

II

Rainbow Weather

Incanting a sound strangely of this world
the boats, low in the harbour,
said all there was to say about ups and downs.
I liked the fact that such a sound is what comes
of a little buffeting, and thought it true to life,
like the rise and fall of blood sugar
I'd call the body's rainbow weather.
It was always one thing after another –
and the only way we could be in the world, you and I,
was when that sound which inhabits
the long afternoon the way salt inhabits air
was more than true to life; when boat, wind
and the music the two made together exemplified
the pneuma, or Paraclete, or something, something
not seen, not visibly created – like dark matter.
Your thought, that is to say, seemed always
to brood above the face of the waters.

We stepped across the causeway for the better part
of the beach. The gulls, you said, were like quavers
detaching from an invisible stave,
sweeping in on us with their horrid recital.
The only way, I said, of dealing with this is –
if you can imagine it – to upturn each crescent moon
that governs the swing of your moods
into a crucible, and start from there, quite scientifically;
study your charts, and watch your compass,

and say to yourself: there is no stain
that cannot dissolve in water,
no clinker of habit, no fixed residue.

By this time we'd drunk the last of the ale.
As you rolled the empty bottle across the tarmac,
it curved inertly on the path of its own barmy ecliptic.
All we could do was make up names
for boats in the harbour:
Antares, *Kyrie*, *The Mazzaroth*;
names suddenly real in the slurring rain.
Arcturus, *Cygnus*, *The God Help Us*;
their hulls like cupped hands, hands of oblation.
Cercylas, *Inebrius*, *The Chimay Blue* –
and that was quite enough; by then I had to shush you.

Balquhidder Road End

Rain makes us quiet inside the house,
unhooks our miscellaneous voices
from their throat-pegs
and fills the loch with them. We look on,

muted, amazed at the full length of our bodies,
our considered reaction to spilt tea,
the circle of chairs, chapters and verses
Blu-Tacked to the far wall.

Renouncing the alphabet, I left the retreat,
took up a pair of long-handled secateurs
and cut down the weeds. The high hollow stems

of the nettles snicked and bowed,
priest-like, shook pollen over my shoes.
Their sting became canticle inside my hand.

Ruth

I saw you in chapel in 'the vanishing village',
Dunino, with a blue armful of barley
and the light shining right through you.
The scribe said your sorrows were *numerous*,
that to leave father, mother and homeland
would translate into kindness, once the heart had calmed.
No mention of grappling with your load
on the road from Moab to Bethlehem; your griefs
held back for Naomi's sake; biting your lip, absently noting
what those tides of desert sand were doing to you.
All this condensed into: *And it came to pass . . .*

And seeing as we were alone there, I asked
about the dark stain of tears and sweat on the fabric
of your dress, the sprain of the mile by mile,
stretching your exilic limbs for those lengths
the widowed have always taught
will be worth it, one way or another, in time.
It seems you'd calculated, clear as glass, the day-in-day-out
gleaning of the harvest would lead up to something.
Yet one more question shines out for the asking:
as you uncovered the feet of your near-kinsman
what was it like, for a change, to *go not empty away?*

A View of Christ in the House of Martha and Mary

(Diego Velázquez)

And within the house, beyond the space
for sitting and eating, beyond
the plate of peeled eggs,
the white paper glove of the undressed clove,

the fish-wet table, the wet, unflinching fish-eyes,
the slowly shrivelling chilli,
there is the otherness of a lit room.
Martha's heart troubles her –

despite all counsel, she would seem
the least blessed, unnourished
in the simple foreground of exclusion,

yet, to our eyes, she is closest,
should we wish to savour what is close;
she is the cynosure, the open invitation.

Gabapentin

(Iceland)

I. 300mg

I remember checking my shoes
at the foot of Vatnajökull,

boarding the bus for the hairpins.
It was '98, and makeshift rituals

could not hold against a glacier's
dark sedated heaps, born of calamity,

barbiturate and edged with a glistening
that must always break, and break away.

How solid it seemed, that thin place,
obliging us our trek through settlements

of cloud and snow, hesitant silence.

II. 600mg

Blowing into my coffee, I recall the fjord
at Akureyri where haar came up to the backdoor

looking like a yawn turned inside out
yet too bright for itself to be tired,

lit with a tearful excess of light.
And as my glasses un-steam

I'm already in a high place, staring vacantly
at where a township used to be.

III. 900 mg

Loss of co-ordination, reduced alertness, reduced ability
to concentrate, involuntary movement of the eyes, shaking.
Loss of memory, problems with speech, pins and needles
or numbness, twitches, changes in reflex reactions, changes
in appetite, unusual thoughts.
　—Patient advice leaflet

There were no roads inland,
only rivers. I forget their names.

Before long I'd capsized into the loaming floss
where those rivers rend themselves

for a mass conversion;
a pagan cantor in a colossal frock

going down with the din –
all of which suggests that Godafoss

still smacks of effigies, the old beards
concealed in their watery temple.

Pulling my weight back onto land,
just as the undescending sun locked

the trolls in rock, I was cut loose from time
to cross the peninsula unhindered.

IV. 1200 mg

[…]

hearing the shutter freeze over
as the camera hit the surface of the sea

saying, *good shot, but leave it to the waves*
to […]

[…]
only its tail in the boreal light […]

Longhand

(S.T.C. to W.W.)

Judging by the handwriting, this man's mind
is as one-pointed as the pen travelling left to right
across the paper, his heart and hand
linked by the same meridian,
as his thoughts appear before him on the page.
It's Tuesday morning, January 1798.
In a few days the addressee will open his letter
with such haste, the word […] is lost forever
in red wax. *Wherever your after residence may be,*
it is probable that you will be within the reach
of my Tether, lengthened as it now is.- - -
The letter's brittle in my hand, as time, uroboric,
weaves its circle of constant longitude.
It's Tuesday morning, January 2002.

The Long View

After a last late breakfast, leaving
my lover to his renovations, meaning
I was out and she was in, I took the old route
past the boarded-up clubs of St Judes,

and in another ten minutes of chewing-gum
walked past the requisite subway bum
and down along by the floating harbour
where, on the other side of the water,

the brewery was being demolished,
and the bricks that once said *Courage*
then said *age*, and then nothing,
gave a perspective more edifying

than anything which until then
I'd maintained as my ground plan.
Coming down to earth meant losing the cause
I'd spent all my years looking for,

deciding, then and there: *better the stranger*
you don't know, for the devil's view is shorter.
And the river-mouth said as much
as it opened out for that longer reach.

Meteor Shower

Lying down on a bench by the sea,
a Taurean moon making its path of light
across the water, I think of you
who I loved not so long ago
for the cappuccino froth in your moustache.

After a while I lose count of the shooting stars,
the radiant dust of the Perseids.
The hour's passed when I said I'd make tracks
and return to the room I call home,
not quite mine, yet no one else's.

Librettist

I've just seen how your eyes reflect
the moon passing through the Zodiac.
At this precise hour they're wider than usual
and would appear to discern more of me:
halfway through the sign of the scales
I note this innovation, this clarity,
how quick they are to collaborate;
though, in all fairness, they seem more at peace
· than mine, and exact the longer harmonies.
I can't sustain my glance, knowing
we'll lose this moment to a change of phase,
secretive and sickle-shaped.

Falls of Inversnaid

I doubt we could say now
that the water thunders down,

but rather, beginning at some spot
of rockrose, moss and bracken,

it *believes*, cannot do other
than turn towards its larger cause

and, from scintillate wit and flaunt
around the dark roll of rock,

come to serve the sober life,
bringing the over and above back down

to where they have meaning
for us – cloud and mountain mood

made equable in the same calm mirror –
until we lose ourselves again

in the lift and fall of the water,
its let-be and lintel of light.

Syzygy

A desire for a house with a glass roof
made me get up and walk the streets
at four in the morning. The full moon was looking
as if she'd passed a loaded remark
at some conference that was drawing to a close.

How strange for the world to have turned
and be facing the other way again.
Why do we sleep through these great rotations?
The night sky sometimes likes a good conversation,
and gives me plenty of time to speak before thinking.

The Canal at Claverton

(Job 13)

Imagine the false comforters waving us off,
still eloquently stammering from their moral maze,
those *physicians of no value* who rant
about the dangers of sleeping on water,

and we'll park up, climb aboard and absorb
this perspective on its articulate clearing,
its gloss and uplift around the prow.
I've said it before, but consider the Fates are with us,

or rather, how they look out from our eyes,
or better still, are nothing but the light
that lives inside our looking, and the trees
that double down towards reed-beds

will parallel the timing
we're just beginning to reach
between your clock and mine.
Say this, and they'll bind us side by side.

Void of Course

The route led along a cycle path,
past the red heart on the tree stump,
and into the orchard of what was
a waiting room, a ticket office,
a time-tabled portal
now clockless and overgrown.
I supposed you wouldn't say *yes*,

but you wouldn't say *no*.
The moon was void of course,
invigilating that hour's impasse
as I thought of your outstretched arms
and another path
I couldn't have planned for,
starting where the platform ended.

Tentsmuir

I

Behind the house the dark roams
in a shape called *forest*.
Alert like a battalion, it's camped
as close as possible to the sea.
Fast becoming its new recruit,
I'm caught at magnetic north
where Tentsmuir tells itself by name,
is nature replete
in her skirt of scrag and sand.
In the *apothēkē*
of a northerly landscape,
more out of reach than ever before,
the road here is purposeful,
must be taken like medicine.

II

Forget the idea of a cure –
what's needed is allegiance,
kneeling by the fire to kindle
an old saying – *therefore can I lack nothing.*
This green acre lightens
a burden magnified by the moon
(I've felt my lips thicken, beak-like,
my eyes become almost lidless
as the landscape puts down
its roots in me). They say
the poison is the promise,
so I must carry my complaint
to the high court of silence,
and rest it there.

III

Losing my way, I'm haunted
from the inside by owl-eyes,
glide and down-sight
of the deft sparrowhawk.
I've grown used to things unknown,
have come to expect them,
like the body in shock,
its lyric lightning,
the vigil in the paradox,
meaning: there's no need
to leave a light on all night –
just be glad for the way these lines
drop like pine needles
silently to the forest floor.

IV

Words returned to with the stub
of a pencil. First light.
Then dark. The drawn curtain
hides the moon and stars,
hides the moon and stars. *Selah*.
Like the beaver, I've built
my burrow with more than one way
in and out. Happier in water,
but not without land in sight.
First forest, consonant and dense,
or store-house, say, like Hebraic text —
so much volume to such small weight.
Heavy lightness . . . feather of lead . . .
dust of gold darkens overhead.

V

To stay under cover
then open out
from cleared ground.
The wind is full of teeth
and works us hard.
Be sustained by the night-speak
of birds, their sounding-out
from the balm
of the listening dark.
Not the obstacle removed,
but the journey through –
blessed *in absentia*
by a light touch,
or something written in sand.

VI

Outgoing in an incoming way,
Tentsmuir washes off on me,
absolves the past
with a more-from-less saltiness.
And slowly, with loose change
for old rope, let the boat out,
let it go; un-mended
but amenable, unwinding
from the taut length.
The bones in the braes have blossomed
by dew of light leaked into them.
I recall conduits of solace,
a sub-croft with a stellate niche –
a star of thorn.

VII

Lungs grow back their forests,
rich in iron and lichen.
I am, I am,
is all that remains –
the old call-notes fail.
I will pick no bones
with the buzzards.
Hast thou considered . . . ?
Tell me:
what should I make
from these potsherds –
a household god?
A mosaic floor?
A path through the trees?

VIII

Your letters come typed,
referring me to Shelley on Keats,
that water might be better
for writing in than sand.
I've looked into your rippling
thought-print, a dark fixative –
and what develops
is the image of Ezekiel,
that look on the prophet's face
as the waters flowed out
from under the threshold
of the Temple.
Is there a smile on his face?
Are his eyebrows raised?

IX

On a night-walk through the forest
rich green scarves
of memory,
silks of the haar,
brush my face –
this would be a slow world
for slow measures
but I move too rapidly –
steps are uneven
between the limbs
of the trees,
until I feel my way
down to the easy sand
of the Eden estuary.

X

For 'Leuchars', read
'place of the rushes'.
Say 'love' is a long wait
for a song played back
from the everlasting –
read 'the heart
is tempted back
to its hiding place'.
Ecclesiastes says,
'Much study
is weariness of the flesh'.
For 'moon', read:
close the book
and look up.

XI

You arrived part way
into the hour. There was something
of the falling of rain
about you, a rook's glossy
mischief slipping through
inchoate dark. You leaned over,
asked what I was writing,
a light sweat above your lips.
How could I have missed you
in a place where bird's feet
are like clusters of keys
I could reach for,
but never grasp –
such is the gravity of the task.

XII

To walk out of the sea
is to make a sound close
to the seal's bark – that bubble-
swallowing, well-rounded
sound of dive and deep.
A gulp against my shins,
heels winged with water,
I push towards the glint
and glean of the strewn shore
where my shoes wait side by side,
dog-sniffed in sunlight.
But to see this place at dusk,
in a high wind, is walk through
an aurora borealis of sand.

XIII

Take the sea mist,
its light-leap, the kissed air,
how it dismisses my plans
to keep doing what I do,
and it's immediately clear:
doubts can be harboured,
the sky does not have to be blue.
Yet, if I didn't pull
every step
from the sand,
nothing would happen,
although what happens here
is nothing but the call
of the sanderling.

XIV

Past the murmured liturgy of cornfields
and into your dark tent of listening:
bird-call like the click
of dripping rain,
or, 'heard in our land', turtle doves
purring their night-night –
summer air, then silence.
How can you not have stayed me?
I will spring from you like an orchid.
You have fed back into yourself
the steps I sought to retrace,
bled from me like resin.
My nadir, root-place,
lay of my homestead.

Already someone's set their dogs among the swans

The loch looks away, up at the crags
of Holyrood Park, as the landscape
turns witness to all that, one day,
I'd be surprised to think of as myself.
My tongue slumps in my mouth again,
a bastard feather. The moon, wearing
her off-the-shoulder number, slips

her bare shadows down to my feet –
my ghost preceding me, like a magnet.
The swans begin to nest, or, snorting water,
turn like hefty lanterns
gazing around themselves
as headlights of late traffic, brash crescendos,
rally for expiring destinations.

For nothing withstands this coolness
closing in, so constantly remote.
I'd live the night out
on the dark hymnal lake, to hear it talking
towards the edges of itself – that voice of the waters
so completely unbothered,
syllabic and out for the count.

Sandpipers

How easy it is to imitate
the sandpipers,
their breasts the same colour
as the breaking waves –
so you'll not see
how I've done this,
but consider it the outcome
of my being off-set
against the same mirrored cuff
of the North Sea
that belongs to you,
but cannot belong to me –
it all happens so quickly,
and to watch these creatures
who without consciousness of self
inhabit eternity, is as closely
aligned as we'll ever be –
so when I've left, remember me
by how light they are
on their legs –
how they look at you
with a tilted head.

Frog Genesis

As if they'd come down clean in vertical weather,
a line of descent straight from the rainstorm,
afterbirth of lightning and thunder,
each a centimetre long, crossing the track.
Little sobrieties, little regenerations,
sickle-green, cold strobes of earth
you watched your step for, scrotum-soft,
hopping into your hand for their first lesson in trust.

You were a coincidence, a meniscus;
human and otherness, above and below,
bent so the curve of your spine sheltered,
your cupped hands offered,
and the word *frogs* asked of you
what smallest thing grew from your grieving?

Ephemeris

And how like us it was
that a freak fall of snow
came to pass comment
on the scene. Not the coffee
and the conversation,
but the parting kiss
and its quick precision

after which not a thought
could come to rest
without losing itself in the next.
And even if one day
tells another, we started
as we meant to go on, in the light
of those elliptical flakes.

Notes

Human Telescope: the title is adapted from a footnote in Richard Holmes' *The Age of Wonder* (London: Harper Press, 2009), p.113.

The Hum: the epigraph is from Osip Mandelstam's 'The Word and Culture', in *The Collected Critical Prose and Letters*, ed. Jane Gary Harris, trans. Jane Gary Harris and Constance Link (London: Collins Harvill, 1991), p.116.

A View of Canaletto's Venice: *Passata sotto* – this is an evasive counterattack in fencing, made by withdrawing the rear leg in a reverse lunge. Literally, 'to pass under'.

Cycle Path: 'Silly Suffolk' is a corruption of 'Selig', meaning 'holy', on account of the vast number of churches in the county, many of which date from before 1086.

The Extra Mile

IV: *'discomfort is corrosive'* – this refers to William Blake's printing technique in *The Marriage of Heaven and Hell*.

V: Elihu is the last and youngest of the 'false comforters' to kindle his wrath against Job. His speech is a later addition to the text.

11 and 22 (thousand) are the sum of Job's livestock at the start and end of the prose framework (Job 1:3, 42:12). There are 22 consonants in the Hebrew alphabet and,

for the Jews, as Norman K. Gottwald observes in *Studies in the Book of Lamentations*, letters 'were thought of as holy, directly breathing the spirit of God.'

Cipher: see Blake's illustrations to *Job*, Plate XI, which depicts the nadir-point in the story.

Ruth: 3:7. 'And when Boaz had eaten and drunk, and his heart was merry, he went to lie down at the end of the heap of corn: and she came softly, and uncovered his feet, and laid her down.'

Gabapentin, III: Godafoss is a waterfall in the north of Iceland. It's said that when Christianity came to Iceland the old pagan effigies were thrown into it.

Tentsmuir, VII: *'Hast thou considered?'* – Job, 2:3.

VIII: Ezekiel, 47.

XIV: *'heard in our land'* – Song of Songs, 2:12.

Acknowledgements

Thanks to the editors of the following magazines and publications in which some of these poems, or versions of them, first appeared:

'Addicted to Brightness' (Long Lunch Press), *Archipelago, Markings, Other Poetry, Poetry Wales,* 'The Captain's Tower: Seventy Poets Celebrate Bob Dylan at Seventy' (Seren), *The Yellow Nib.*

Grateful acknowledgements are due also to The Gray's Trust Kersey, The Harold Hyam Wingate Foundation, and the University of St Andrews Student Support Services, for financial assistance.